How to Draw the Life and Times of
George W. Bush

Roderic Schmidt

The Rosen Publishing Group's
PowerKids Press™
New York

To Evelyn

Published in 2006 by The Rosen Publishing Group, Inc.
29 East 21st Street, New York, NY 10010

First Edition

Editor: Amelie von Zumbusch and Rachel O'Connor
Layout Design: Elana Davidian
Photo Researcher: Jeffrey Wendt

Illustrations: All illustrations by Albert Hanner.
Photo Credits: p. 4 © Corbis Sygma; p. 7 © Brooks Kraft/Corbis; p. 8 © Brooks Kraft/Corbis;
p. 9 Ronald Martinez/Getty Images; p. 10 © David Reiman; p. 14 © Martin H. Simon/Corbis; p. 16
© Joseph Sohm; ChromoSohm Inc./Corbis; p. 18 © Bettmann/Corbis; p. 20 © Tribune Media Services;
p. 22 Paul J. Richards/AFP/Getty Images; p. 24 © 2002 R&N 21 Jewelers, Inc.; p. 26 Library of
Congress Geography and Map Division; p. 28 White House Photo Office.

Library of Congress Cataloging-in-Publication Data

Schmidt, Roderic.
  How to draw the life and times of George W. Bush / Roderic Schmidt.
     p. cm. — (A kid's guide to drawing the presidents of the United States of America)
  Includes index.
  ISBN 1-4042-3019-X (library binding)
  1. Bush, George W. (George Walker), 1946– —Juvenile literature. 2. Presidents—United States—
Biography—Juvenile literature. 3. Drawing—Technique—Juvenile literature. I. Title. II. Series.
  E903.S34 2006
  973.931092—dc22

                                   2005028981

Printed in China

Contents

A Winding Path to the White House

George Walker Bush is the forty-third president of the United States. He was born in New Haven, Connecticut, on July 6, 1946, to George H. W. Bush and Barbara Pierce Bush. George H. W. Bush served as America's forty-first president from 1989 to  1992. Barbara Bush is related to the fourteenth president, Franklin Pierce.

When George was two years old, his family moved from Connecticut to Odessa, Texas. The Bushes moved several times, settling in Midland, Texas, in 1950.

Bush followed in his father and grandfather's footsteps, attending Phillips Academy and later Yale University. He was good at organizing the other students for games and activities. After graduating from Yale, he served in the Texas Air National Guard. He went back to school and earned a masters degree in business administration, or MBA, from Harvard Business School in 1975. Bush then returned to Texas. There he entered the oil business and married Laura Welch.

His oil business was not a great success, but Bush turned out to be a great help in getting his father elected president in 1988. In 1989, he organized the purchase of the Texas Rangers baseball team. He managed the team successfully until 1994, when he left to run for governor of Texas. He won the election and was reelected in 1998. In 2000, he ran for president and won.

You will need the following supplies to draw the life and times of George W. Bush:

✓ A sketch pad ✓ An eraser ✓ A pencil ✓ A ruler

These are some of the shapes and drawing terms you need to know:

Horizontal Line	—	Squiggly Line	∿
Oval	⬭	Trapezoid	⏢
Rectangle	▭	Triangle	△
Shading	▰	Vertical Line	│
Slanted Line	/	Wavy Line	∼

President and Son of a President

Six weeks after Election Day, the Supreme Court declared George W. Bush the winner of the 2000 election. Bush is only the second man to become president after his father. The first was John Quincy Adams. Adams was elected in 1824, 28 years after his father, John Adams, served as president.

Early on in his presidency, Bush worked on reducing taxes and improving education at home. He also worked to reduce the number of U.S. soldiers stationed overseas.

After terrorists attacked the United States on September 11, 2001, President Bush's main goal was to keep the United States safe from terrorism. He worked to make the United States safer with the Homeland Security Act. He sent U.S. troops to Afghanistan in 2001 and to Iraq in 2003 to defeat terrorists and their allies.

In 2004, President Bush was reelected. He promised to continue to fight terrorism both in the United States and around the world.

On March 18, 2004, President Bush welcomed U.S. soldiers to Fort Campbell in Kentucky. The soldiers were returning from the war in Iraq. He told them, "You have helped keep America safe. You make us all proud to be Americans."

Bush's Texas

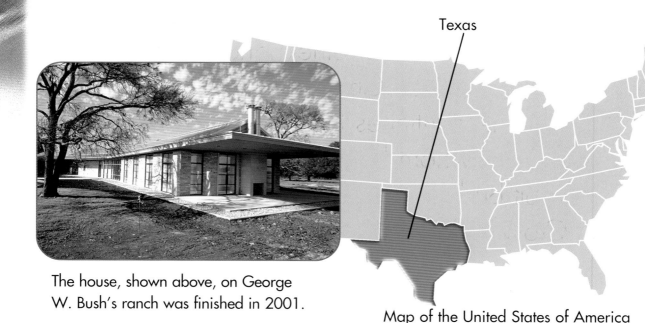

Texas

The house, shown above, on George W. Bush's ranch was finished in 2001.

Map of the United States of America

Texas has a very proud history. It was an independent country, the Republic of Texas, from 1836 until 1845, when it joined the United States. Many Texans are still very independent and like doing things on their own. Two presidents, Dwight D. Eisenhower and Lyndon B. Johnson, were born in Texas.

Although George W. Bush was born in Connecticut, he considers himself a Texan. George was young when his family moved to Odessa, Texas, in 1948. His father went to work in the oil business there. The Bushes spent part of 1949 in

California and then finally settled in Midland, Texas, the following year. The Bushes became very involved in Midland life. They formed close bonds with people in their neighborhood. They watched each other's children, played sports together, and went to services at the First Presbyterian Church. Bush loved growing up in Texas. He continues to be friends with some of the people with whom he grew up in Midland.

As an adult Bush purchased a 1,600-acre (647 ha) ranch in Crawford, Texas. He enjoys going to the ranch to relax with his family, to fish, and to enjoy the canyons, waterfalls, and wildlife of the area. He has met with leaders from other nations there. Some of the people who live in Crawford have joked that Bush's ranch is the "southwest wing" of the White House.

The people of Crawford, Texas, honored Bush with this sign. Bush bought the Prairie Chapel Ranch in Crawford in 1999.

Bush as a Child

When George W. Bush was born in 1946, his family was just beginning to build their fortune. The family lived in a Yale dormitory for married  students at 37 Hillhouse Avenue in New Haven, Connecticut. The Bushes were three of the 40 people living in a house that had been built for one family! The building, shown here, is still used by Yale University.

George had two sisters and three brothers. The Bushes suffered a great loss, however, in 1953. That year Bush's sister Robin died at age three. He tried to cheer his parents up over the loss of his sister. Many family friends say that Bush's light-hearted, joking manner dates from this time.

Bush was active in many sports, but Little League baseball was his favorite. He was popular in grade school. He was energetic and sometimes got into trouble for harmless jokes.

1

As a baby George W. Bush lived at 37 Hillhouse Avenue in New Haven, Connecticut. Begin your drawing of the house by making a rectangular guide.

2

Draw a trapezoid in the middle of the rectangular guide. Draw a horizontal line on each side of it. Add three curved lines below the trapezoid as shown.

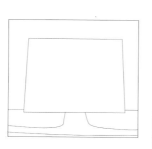

3

Add two horizontal lines and four slanted lines above the trapezoid. Draw a rectangle and a trapezoid connected by two vertical lines. Add five windows. The upper windows are more curved than the lower windows.

4

Erase any extra lines. Draw the steps as shown. Look carefully at the drawing. Add details around and in the top middle window. Draw the door as shown. Add the details around the door.

5

Add the details around and in the four outer windows. Add two vertical and two horizontal lines to the house. Look carefully at the drawing. Add the details to the roof as shown.

6

Draw a small square on the bottom right corner of the house. Use slanted and horizontal lines to draw the stones in the path in front of the house.

7

Use squiggly lines to draw the plants in front of the house.

8

Erase any extra lines. Finish the drawing with shading. The bottom level of the house, the stairs, and the roof are the darkest parts.

The Education of George W. Bush

In 1961, George W. Bush went to Phillips Academy in Andover, Massachusetts. His grades were average, but he became the head cheerleader. His charm and ability to make

friends easily made him very popular. In 1964, Bush went to Yale University. He spent much of his time there enjoying life and getting involved in good-natured mischief with the other members of Delta Kappa Epsilon, a fraternity he had joined.

Bush joined the Texas Air National Guard in 1968. He learned to fly F-102 fighter planes. While serving in the National Guard, he helped his father run for Senate in 1970. He was honorably discharged from the National Guard in 1973. He did not have to see combat, or battle. Bush decided to get an MBA from Harvard Business School. He finished his degree in 1975 and then returned to Midland to get involved in the oil business.

1 On page 12, you can see the seal of Delta Kappa Epsilon, the fraternity of which Bush was a member at Yale. To begin your drawing of the fraternity's seal, make a rectangular guide as shown.

2 Draw a triangle inside the rectangular guide. Draw a small circle as shown. Draw two vertical lines below the triangle. Add two curved lines connecting the vertical lines. Draw four slanted lines.

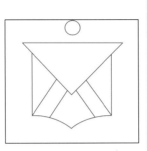

3 Use curved and squiggly lines to draw the wings on each side of the small circle. Draw the shield as shown. Add two slanted lines. Use wavy lines to draw the ribbon as shown.

4 Erase extra lines. Add two hearts as shown. Draw a sideways teardrop shape above the shield. Add a thick upside-down *V* to the right side of the shield. Carefully draw the lion on the left.

5 Draw a rectangle with semicircles on each side of it below the shield. Add curved lines connecting the semicircles to the hearts. Add details to the eye above the shield. Add the lines around the eye.

6 Erase extra lines. Draw three stars below the upside-down *V*. Above the upside-down *V*, draw two crossed slanted lines. Add two triangles to the lines. Add four slanted lines and two triangles.

7 Look carefully at the drawing and write the Greek letters as shown. In English they mean "Friends from the Heart, Forever."

8 Finish your drawing with shading. The lion and the upside-down *V* should be the darkest parts.

Laura Bush

When George W. Bush returned to Midland in 1975, he worked as a landman in the oil business. As a landman he would try to lease, or rent, the oil rights from landowners who had rights to the oil under various pieces of land. He had little money to start with

but made up for that disadvantage with hard work. Two years after moving back to Texas, Bush met Laura Welch. It was love at first sight. Laura had also grown up in Midland, but their paths had not crossed before. They married just three months after they first met.

Laura taught elementary school from 1968 to 1972. She earned a master's degree in library science in 1973. Then she worked as a children's librarian until she married Bush. Laura is still interested in education. She is involved in programs in the United States and overseas that seek to bring education to more people.

1

The picture of Laura Bush on page 14 was taken in the White House in 2001. Make a rectangular guide to begin your drawing of First Lady Laura Bush.

2

Draw an oval guide for her head. Use slanted lines to draw guides for her body, her arms, and her hands. Draw the chair arm her hands are resting on as shown. Add a vertical line.

3

Erase all extra lines. Use the guides from step 2 to draw her hands. Make sure to draw her ring. Draw the shapes of her ear, her neck, and her face. Draw the wavy V of her shirt.

4

Draw three circles and two curved lines as guides for her nose, her eyes, and her mouth. Add a curved line for her earring.

5

Draw the shapes of her hair and clothes with wavy lines. Use the guides to draw her eyes, her nose, her mouth, and her eyebrows. Add lines to her face and ear as shown.

6

Erase any extra lines. Look at the drawing to see which lines need to be erased.

7

Add wavy lines to show the waves in her hair. Add more wavy lines to show the folds in her clothes. Add lines to her eyes as shown.

8

Finish your drawing of Laura Bush with shading. Her mouth, her hair, her eyebrows, and the inside of her eyes should be the darkest parts.

A Texan Businessman

In 1978, George W. Bush ran for Congress but did not get elected. This was upsetting to Bush, but it gave him experience in running a political campaign. Bush continued his work in the oil business even while he was getting involved in politics. He formed an oil-exploration company called Arbusto in

1977. He had success with the company in the 1970s, but less success in the 1980s. In 1986, he managed to sell his oil business for a large profit.

In 1989, Bush used the profits from the sale to become a part owner of the Texas Rangers baseball team. He worked as a manager of the team until 1994. He helped get a new stadium, the Ballpark in Arlington, built for the team. The stadium, now called the Ameriquest Field, is regarded as one of the best in the world. Bush was part owner until 1998, when he sold his share of the team.

1

The photo on page 16 was taken on April 18, 1998. That day, the Texas Rangers played the Baltimore Orioles. Begin your drawing of the Ballpark in Arlington with a rectangular guide.

2

Look carefully at the drawing. Draw a wavy line as shown for the edge of the baseball field.

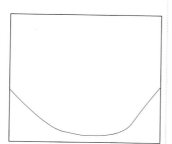

3

Draw a horizontal line across the top of the rectangular guide. Below the horizontal line, draw a curved line as shown.

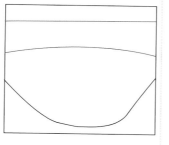

4

Draw a diamond with two curved ends. Add an oval inside it. Draw a curved line above it. Add curved and slanted lines to the curved line as shown. Draw the shape below the diamond.

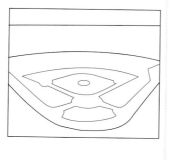

5

Draw the four slanted shapes at the bottom of the rectangular guide. Look carefully at the drawing. Add the shapes to the left. Then draw the shapes to the right.

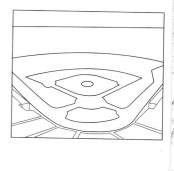

6

Draw eight rectangles. Add lines to make a rectangle to the right. Draw the seats along the field with vertical and slanted lines. Add vertical, horizontal, and slightly curved lines as shown.

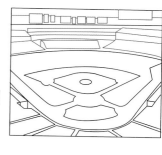

7

Add a small diamond as shown. It is home plate.

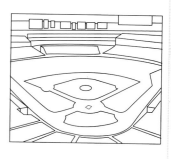

8

Shade in your drawing of the stadium. Home plate should be dark. The spaces between the seats should also be dark.

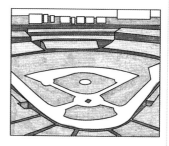

Governor of the Lone Star State

George W. Bush helped his father run for president in 1988. His father won, and, in 1992, Bush helped with the reelection campaign. When his father was defeated, Bush began to consider running for governor of Texas as a Republican. Bush was well known because of his family name and his management of the Texas Rangers. After a close campaign in 1994, Bush defeated the popular governor, Ann Richards.

As governor Bush worked to improve education in Texas. He also made Texas more welcoming to big businesses, so they would move there and hire more Texans. He increased punishment for crimes and made it easier for Texans to carry guns to protect themselves. Bush's charm and skill at getting along with people made him a popular governor. He was reelected by a large majority in 1998. After Bush won such a big victory in Texas, many people began to think that Bush would make a good Republican candidate for president.

1

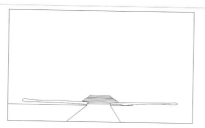

The picture on page 18 shows the Texas Governor's Mansion, or house. Bush lived there while he was governor of Texas. Start your drawing by making a rectangular guide.

2

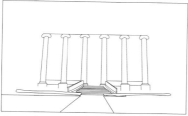

Draw two slanted lines at the bottom of the rectangular guide. Add a horizontal line and two wavy horizontal shapes as shown. Draw the eight steps leading up to the house.

3

Use slanted and vertical lines to draw the walls along the stairs. Add a horizontal line. Draw six columns below the horizontal line. Add lines between the bases of the columns.

4

Add four more horizontal lines above the columns. Add small vertical lines and slanted lines to these horizontal lines. Draw more horizontal lines between the columns.

5

Draw the door and seven windows. Add rectangles for shutters as shown. Draw the lines and shapes around the door. Add two ovals to the door. Add lines to the windows.

6

Look closely at the drawing. Draw the large tree on the left as shown. Add the bushes to the left side of the house. Draw the trees in the background on the left.

7

Erase all extra lines. Draw the bushes on the right side of the house. Look carefully at the drawing. Draw the tree to the right side of the house.

8

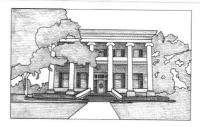

Finish your drawing of the Governor's Mansion with shading. You can leave the columns and the path leading up to the house white.

The 2000 Presidential Election

George W. Bush ran for president in 2000, and he defeated Democrat Albert Gore Jr. However, Bush won under unusual conditions. Gore and Bush had almost

the same number of votes in Florida. Many of the ballots had problems that made it hard to figure out for whom the vote had been cast. It looked like there would be many recounts, with Gore winning some and Bush winning others. About one month after the election, the Supreme Court got involved. The Court decided that Bush had won Florida's electoral votes.

In a presidential election, each state has a certain number of electoral votes. The candidate who wins most of the votes in a state gets all that state's electoral votes. The candidate who wins the most electoral votes overall wins the presidency. By winning Florida's votes, Bush had enough electoral votes to win the election. However, more people nationwide had voted for Gore. This means that Gore won the popular vote but lost the election.

1 Steve Sack drew this political cartoon making fun of both the Republicans and the Democrats. It was printed in the *Minneapolis Star-Tribune*. Begin your drawing of the cartoon with a rectangular guide.

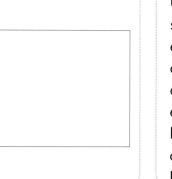

2 Use slanted lines to draw two trapezoids as shown. They look like rectangles, but their right sides are longer than their left sides.

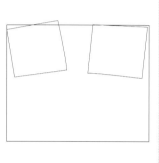

3 Draw sticks for signs. Look carefully at the drawing. Use slanted lines to draw guides for the elephant and the donkey as shown. The donkey is on the left and the elephant is on the right.

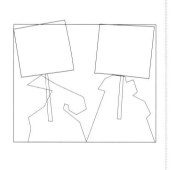

4 Use the guide from step 3 to draw the donkey. Pay special attention to the donkey's nose and arm. The donkey stands for the Democrats. Donkeys often stand for the Democratic Party.

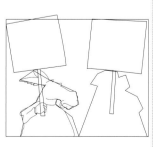

5 Use the guide from step 3 to draw the elephant. Make sure to draw its hand, its arm, and its trunk. The elephant stands for the Republicans. Elephants often stand for the Republican Party.

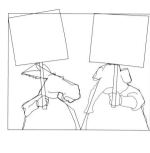

6 Add eyes to the elephant and the donkey as shown. Draw lines to show their lowered arms. Add lines to their faces and their bodies as shown. Add a small circle to the donkey's nose.

7 Write the words as shown. The Republicans want the recount to end because they are afraid they will lose. The Democrats want it to go on until they get enough votes to win.

8 Use shading to finish your drawing. The cartoon is saying that both the Democrats and the Republicans are more worried about beating each other than about finding out who really won the election.

21

A Compassionate Conservative President

During his campaign George W. Bush said that he was a compassionate conservative. As a conservative Bush believes that the government should not be very involved in people's lives. When he became president, Bush reduced environmental protection laws so that businesses could make more money. When businesses do well, they hire more people and spend money in the local community. Another example of Bush's conservatism is his support for major tax cuts. Bush and other conservatives believe that people getting to keep and spend their own money is better for the country than if the government takes their money through taxes and spends it on government programs.

An example of Bush's compassionate side is the No Child Left Behind program. The program aims to improve education in U.S. schools. The program was made law in 2002. It requires that certain basic skills be taught to students and that most of the students in a school pass a test on those skills.

1

The picture on page 22 shows Bush talking about the No Child Left Behind program at a school in St. Louis, Missouri. The picture over Bush's head is the No Child Left Behind logo. Begin your drawing of the logo with a rectangular guide.

2

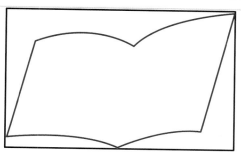

Draw two slanted lines. Draw two curved lines connecting the slanted lines at the top as shown. Add two more curved lines connecting them at the bottom. You have made the book shape of the No Child Left Behind logo.

3

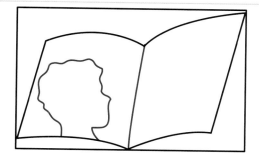

Add one more slanted line to show the middle fold of the book. Look carefully at the drawing. Make the shape of the child's head as shown. The child's hair is to the left. The child's face is to the right.

4

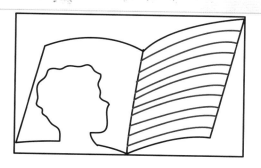

Erase any extra lines. Add 10 curved lines to the right side of the logo. These lines make stripes that look like the stripes on the American flag.

5

Add three stars to the left side of the logo as shown. The stars look like the stars on an American flag.

6

Now shade in your drawing of the No Child Left Behind logo. The top stripe should be dark. After that there is a white stripe. Then there is another dark stripe. The pattern continues and ends with a dark stripe.

September 11, 2001

On September 11, 2001, Al Qaeda terrorists attacked the United States. The terrorists took over four planes. They flew two of the planes into the twin towers of the World Trade Center in New York City, causing the  buildings to fall. They flew another plane into the Pentagon in Washington, D.C. The fourth plane crashed in Pennsylvania after its passengers fought the terrorists. About 3,000 people were killed in the attacks. Americans were deeply shocked and saddened. Countries around the world expressed great sympathy for the United States.

Bush responded to the attacks by declaring a war on terror. Many nations agreed that terrorism was a major problem and wanted to help. The United States would lead them in fighting terrorists and nations that supported terrorists. Bush also created the Department of Homeland Security to organize the fight against terrorism in America.

1

The pin on page 24 was made in memory of the people who died in the September 11 attacks. Begin your own drawing of the pin by making a rectangular guide.

2 Draw a pentagon, or five-sided shape. Inside it add a smaller pentagon. The pin has five sides because the Pentagon, a five-sided military building in Washington D.C., was attacked on September 11.

3

Add four slanted lines at the top of the pentagon. Add four slanted lines to the pentagon's left side. Add four slanted lines to the right side. Draw the shape at the bottom.

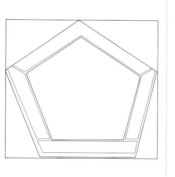

4

Use wavy lines to draw the shape of the flag. Use four slanted lines and three horizontal lines to make the shapes of the two towers of the World Trade Center.

5

Add a star at the pentagon's top. Add stars to the left and right sides of the Pentagon as shown. Add 40 windows to each tower.

6

Add wavy lines to make the 13 stripes on the American flag. Make five rows of six circles each for the stars. A real flag has 50 stars, but only 30 will fit here.

7

Write "AMERICA" on the top left side of the pentagon. Write "UNITED" on the top right side. Write "SEPT. 11, 2001" on the bottom.

8

Shade in your drawing of the September 11 memorial pin. Make the stripes on the flag by shading in only every other stripe as shown.

War in Afghanistan and Iraq

George W. Bush ordered the capture of Osama bin Laden, the leader of Al Qaeda, as the first part of the war on terror. Bin Laden was in Afghanistan, but the Taliban would not give him up to the United  States. On October 7, 2001, America began military operations in Afghanistan. Small numbers of American soldiers helped Afghans overthrow the Taliban by early 2002. However, they did not find Bin Laden.

Bush believed that Saddam Hussein, the leader of Iraq, was helping Al Qaeda. Bush also believed that Hussein had weapons of mass destruction. To continue the war on terror, in October 2002, Congress authorized Bush to attack Iraq if Hussein did not turn over his weapons. When Hussein did not hand over any weapons, the U.S. attacked Iraq in March 2003. On May 1, 2003, Bush declared that major combat was over in Iraq and that America would help rebuild Iraq as a democracy. However, fighting continues in Iraq today.

1

The map on page 26 is of Iraq. Make a large rectangle to begin your own map of Iraq. It should be a little bit taller than it is long. The rectangle will be the guide for your drawing.

2

Look carefully at the drawing. Use the guide to make a rough outline of the country of Iraq.

3

Look carefully at the drawing. Then use the guide from step 2 to draw the borders of the northern part of Iraq.

4

Use the guide from step 2 to draw the borders of the southern part of Iraq. You can look at the drawing for help.

5

Baghdad

Erase any extra lines, including the rectangular guide. Look carefully at the drawing. Make a dot to show the city of Baghdad. Write "Baghdad" under the dot. Baghdad is the capital of Iraq.

6

Baghdad

Shade in your map of Iraq. Iran is to the east of Iraq. Saudi Arabia and Kuwait are to the south. Syria and Jordan are to the west, and Turkey is to the north.

Reelection and a Second Term

In 2004, George W. Bush ran for reelection. Some people were happy with the way Bush was running the war on terror. However, the continued fighting in Iraq upset many other people. After a close campaign, Bush beat John Kerry, the Democratic candidate. In this election Bush got the majority of both the popular and electoral votes.

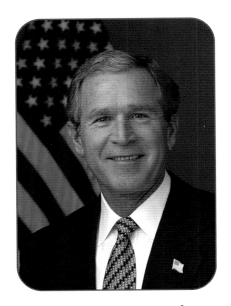

During his second term, Bush has continued to fight the war on terror. He is committed to rebuilding Iraq as a democracy. He believes that a democratic Iraq will be a great help in the war on terror. At home Bush has been working to change Social Security, which is the government program that makes sure older citizens have at least some money on which to live.

The United States is facing many challenges at home and overseas at the beginning of the twenty-first century. George W. Bush continues to meet these challenges head-on.

1

Eric Draper took this picture of President George W. Bush. It was taken at the White House. Make a rectangular guide to begin your drawing of George W. Bush.

2

Draw an oval as a guide for Bush's head. Add six slanted lines to make the guides for his neck, his shoulders, and his body.

3

Add three circles and a line as guides for his eyes, his nose, and his mouth. Draw his hair, his neck, and his ears with wavy lines. Draw his jacket with five wavy lines.

4

Use the guides to draw his eyes, his eyebrows, his nose, and his mouth. Add lines to his face, his ears, and his neck as shown.

5

Draw the collar of his jacket. Add lines for his shirt collar and his tie. Add stripes to his tie with squiggly lines. Draw the flag pin on his jacket.

6

Erase any extra lines. Look at the drawing to figure out which lines need to be erased.

7

Add wavy lines to show the waves in his hair. Add two slanted lines to his flag pin as shown. Draw small lines to show his teeth.

8

Finish your drawing of President George W. Bush with shading. The stripes in his tie, the middle of his eyes, and the top corner of his flag pin should be the darkest parts.

Timeline

1946 George Walker Bush is born on July 6, to George Herbert Walker Bush and Barbara Pierce Bush.

1950 The Bush family settles in Midland, Texas.

1961 Bush enters Phillips Academy in Andover, Massachusetts.

1964 Bush goes to Yale University.

1968 Bush graduates from Yale and joins the Texas Air National Guard.

1973 Bush is honorably discharged from the Texas Air National Guard and enters Harvard Business School.

1975 Bush returns to Midland, Texas.

1977 Bush meets and marries Laura Welch.

1978 Bush unsuccessfully runs for Congress.

1981 Bush's daughters, Barbara and Jenna Bush, are born on November 25.

1989 Bush becomes part owner and manager of the Texas Rangers baseball team.

1994 Bush becomes governor of Texas.

1998 Bush is reelected governor by a large number of votes.

2000 Bush is elected president of the United States.

2001 Al Qaeda attacks the United States on September 11.

2004 Bush is reelected president.

Glossary

allies (A-lyz) Countries or groups that support one another.

ballots (BA-luts) Pieces of paper used in voting.

campaign (kam-PAYN) A plan to get a certain result, such as to win an election.

compassionate (kum-PA-shuh-nut) Showing kindness.

conservative (kun-SER-vuh-tiv) Someone who follows familiar styles.

declared (dih-KLAYRD) Announced officially.

defeated (dih-FEET-ed) Won against someone in a contest or battle.

degree (dih-GREE) A title given to a person who has finished a course of study.

democracy (dih-MAH-kruh-see) A government that is run by the people who live under it.

Democrat (DEH-muh-krat) A person who belongs to the Democratic Party, one of the two major political parties in the United States.

dormitory (DOR-mih-tor-ee) A large building where many people live together.

environmental (en-vy-ern-MEN-tehl) Relating to all the living things and conditions of a place.

fraternity (fruh-TER-nuh-tee) A group of men who share a common interest.

honorably discharged (AH-ner-uh-blee dis-CHARJD) Let out of the armed services with a satisfactory record.

involved (in-VOLVD) Kept busy by something.

ranch (RANCH) A large farm for raising cattle, horses, or sheep.

republic (rih-PUH-blik) A country that has a government in which the authority belongs to the people.

Republican (rih-PUH-blih-ken) A person belonging to the Republican Party, one of the two major political parties in the United States.

Supreme Court (suh-PREEM KORT) The highest court in the United States.

Taliban (TAL-ih-ban) The political party that governed Afghanistan from 1996 to 2002.

terrorists (TER-er-ists) People who use strong force to scare others.

Index

Web Sites

Due to the changing nature of Internet links, PowerKids Press has developed an online list of Web sites related to the subject of this book. This site is updated regularly. Please use this link to access the list:
www.powerkidslinks.com/kgdpusa/gwbush/